GREATEST SPORTS HEROES

Hockey Stars

Therese Shea

HIGH interest books

Children's Press®
A Division of Scholastic Inc.
New York / Toronto / London / Auckland / Sydney
Mexico City / New Delhi / Hong Kong
Danbury, Connecticut

Book Design: Dean Galiano
Contributing Editor: Karl Bollers
Photo Credits: Cover © Al Bello/Getty Images, Inc.; pp. 4, 32, 35 © Jim McIsaac/
Getty Images, Inc.; pp. 7, 22 © Elsa/Getty Images, Inc.; p. 8 © Andy Marlin/Getty
Images, Inc.; p. 11 © Eliot J. Schechter/Getty Images, Inc.; pp. 14, 21, 25 © Dave
Sandford/Getty Images, Inc.; p. 18 © Scott Cunningham/Getty Images, Inc.; p. 28 ©
Harry How/Getty Images, Inc.; pp. 31, 36, 40 © Brian Bahr/Getty Images, Inc.

Library of Congress Cataloging-in-Publication Data

Shea, Therese.
Hockey stars/by Therese Shea.
p. cm.—(Greatest sports heroes)
Includes index.
ISBN-10: 0-531-12587-4 (lib. bdg.)   0-531-18704-7 (pbk.)
ISBN-13: 978-0-531-12587-8 (lib. bdg.)   978-0-531-18704-3 (pbk.)
1. Hockey players—Biography—Juvenile literature. 2. National Hockey League—
Juvenile literature. I. Title. II. Series.

GV848.5.A1.S54 2007
796.962092'2—dc22

2006008052

1 2 3 4 5 6 7 8 9 10 R 11 10 09 08 07

5/0 +

Contents

Introduction

The score is tied, 2–2. The final period of the game has ended and the Cougars and the Boxers are in overtime. Whichever team scores first will win the state championship. The Cougars' left wing has the puck. He skates around the rink, powering toward the goal. The Boxers' goalie gets ready for the goal attempt. He watches to see where the left wing will try to score.

The Boxers' defenseman is covering the attacking left wing. The left wing swipes at the puck with his stick. He moves and the defenseman follows. The defenseman steals the puck. The left wing trips the defenseman with his stick and a penalty is called. The Cougars' left wing is sent to the penalty box. The Cougars will be down one man for the next 2 minutes. Now it is time for the Boxers to make a power play.

Superstar goalie Martin Brodeur of the New Jersey Devils clears the puck in a 2006 game against the Pittsburgh Penguins.

The centers face off. The Boxers get the puck. If they work fast, they can win the game. The Boxers' center passes the puck to his right wing. The right wing speeds along the ice, dodging the other team's defenders. He passes the puck back to the center. For a moment, the puck is loose and a Cougar defenseman takes possession. The center checks the defenseman, however, and regains control of the puck.

The time on the penalty is running out. There are only 20 seconds left to make a power play goal before the penalized player returns to the ice. The Boxers' right and left wings swarm the goal. The center charges toward it and dekes past a defenseman by pretending to pass it to the left. Instead, he pulls his stick back for a slap shot. He connects and the puck goes flying through the air. The goalie throws himself in front of the net, but it is too late. The puck goes in. The game is over. The Boxers are the champions!

Jarome Iginla of the Calgary Flames heads for the net against Christian Backman of the St. Louis Blues.

Great hockey players have awesome skills like speed, power, stamina, and agility. Who are today's top professional hockey stars with these amazing abilities—and how did they become the great players they are? Let's meet eight of today's greats and find out!

7

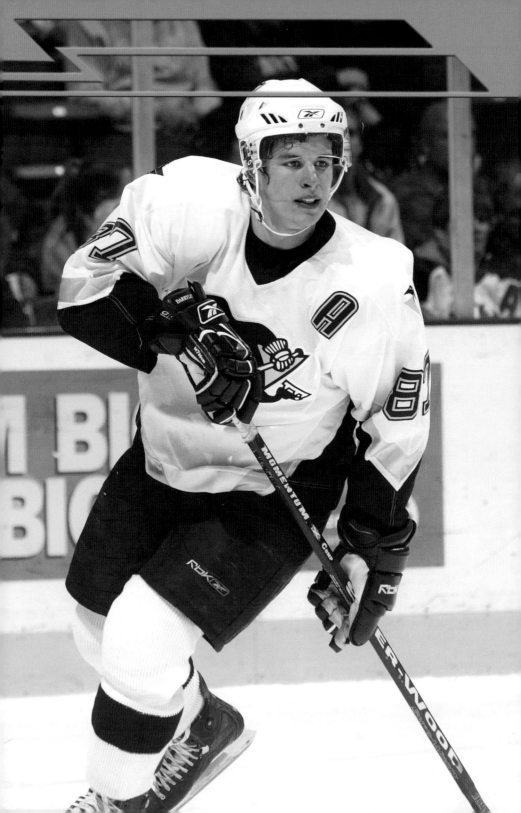

"Sid the Kid." "The Next One." "A National Treasure." "The Gift." These names have all been used to describe Sidney Crosby, a center for the Pittsburgh Penguins in the National Hockey League (NHL). Although young, Sidney is quickly becoming one of the most well-known players in the game.

Sid the Kid

Sidney was born August 7, 1987, in Halifax, Nova Scotia, in Canada. He grew up loving hockey. He started ice skating when he was three years old. His father even painted the basement of their home to look like a hockey rink.

In 2002, Sidney wanted to play for the Québec Major Junior Hockey League (QMJHL), in the Canadian Hockey League (CHL), a major league for fifteen to twenty year olds. Sidney was too young, however. He decided to

"Sid the Kid" Crosby looks for a pass from a teammate in a game against the New Jersey Devils.

attend school and play hockey in the United States for a year. In 2002, he went to Shattuck-St. Mary's School in Minnesota. He scored 72 goals in fifty-seven games in his first year there. He helped the school team win the national title.

In the QMJHL

The next year, Sidney was able to play for the QMJHL. In many leagues, teams get to choose new players in a process called a draft. He was selected first in the draft by the Rimouski Océanic. He was named Rookie of the Year and Player of the Year of the CHL. He scored the most points ever by a sixteen-year-old in the QMJHL.

Player Stats

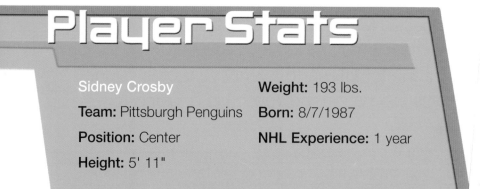

Sidney Crosby

Team: Pittsburgh Penguins

Position: Center

Height: 5' 11"

Weight: 193 lbs.

Born: 8/7/1987

NHL Experience: 1 year

Sidney plays the puck as an opponent moves in from behind in a game against the Florida Panthers.

Sidney didn't slow down during the 2004–2005 season for the Océanic. He scored 66 goals and had 102 assists, leading his team to win the QMJHL championship. He again had the most points in the CHL and was named Player of the Year. Sidney had shown that he was ready to play in the NHL.

Super Rookie

In the 2005 NHL Entry Draft, Sidney Crosby was picked first overall by the Pittsburgh Penguins in the first round. NHL fans everywhere had heard about his talent. Many felt that he was the kind of player who could get fans excited about the sport of hockey again. This was especially important following a lockout that cancelled the entire 2004–2005 season.

Fun Facts

The player to score the most points in a single CHL season was Wayne Gretzky with 182 points in sixty-four games in the 1977–78 season. When asked which player could break his records, Wayne answered, "Sidney Crosby!"

Sidney has quickly become one of the top players in the NHL. After playing for only two months, he led the Penguins in points. He was even named alternate captain of the Penguins in December 2005. People's expectations for Sidney are high. So far, he has met them.

Helping Out

Sidney has helped with many charity events in his lifetime. While in Pittsburgh, he has already participated in several events. In one annual event, Sidney went shopping with a local child. He helped that child pick out a winter coat, boots, gloves, a hat, and a jersey—things the child's family could not afford. Sidney said of this experience, "This was really fun and different…. Having a winter jacket shouldn't be a luxury. People take so much for granted, so it's nice to be able to help these kids. To see how happy it made them is amazing."

Chapter Two

Alexander Ovechkin

Washington Capital, Alex Ovechkin can be both physical and graceful. He has the power to be a top-notch defenseman and the agility to score well in difficult situations. In one January 2006 game, Alex was pushed onto his back by a Phoenix Coyotes defenseman, facing away from the goal. Somehow he managed to hook the puck into the net. This kind of talent is what has made him a star in his rookie year.

The Ovechkin Family

Alex was born September 17, 1985, in Moscow, Russia, to athletic parents. His father played professional soccer. His mother won two Olympic gold medals playing basketball for her country. He calls her his first coach. "My mom was a great sportsman," he says. "She taught me a lot."

Alex started playing hockey at age seven. He became involved with the youth teams of

Alexander skates against the Toronto Maple Leafs in a 2006 game played in Ontario, Canada.

15

the Russian Moscow Dynamo hockey club. The Russian Moscow Dynamo is part of the Russian Super League, the top ice hockey league in Russia. The Super League is the top ice hockey league in Russia. The Russian Moscow Dynamo hockey club has schools and teams for young players. In the 2001–2002 season, Alex scored 26 points in nineteen games on the Dynamo youth team. He was soon invited onto the senior team at age sixteen.

Alex played in international games as well. At the Under-20 World Junior Championships, Alex scored 2 hat tricks and 1 assist. His team took the gold medal. This performance caught the attention of the senior Russian National Team. He was invited to join and became the youngest player ever to score with the team.

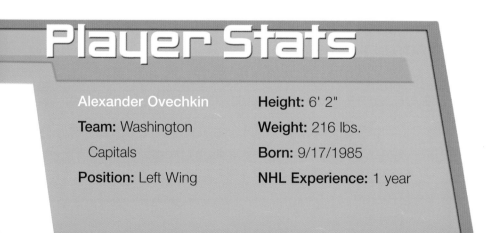

Player Stats

Alexander Ovechkin

Team: Washington Capitals

Position: Left Wing

Height: 6' 2"

Weight: 216 lbs.

Born: 9/17/1985

NHL Experience: 1 year

Dreams of the NHL

Alex had great success with both his Russian professional and national teams. If Alex had stayed in Russia, he could have played for more money. However, he wanted to play in the NHL. Alex said, "The NHL was my dream when I was young. Money is money, but a dream is a dream." In the 2004 hockey draft, he was picked first overall in the first round by the Washington Capitals. Unfortunately, due to the 2004–2005 NHL lockout, Alex did not play with the NHL until the 2005–2006 season.

When the NHL started playing again, Alex was ready. On October 5, he scored 2 goals in his first game and scored at least 1 point in the next eight games. He was Rookie of the Month for December 2005. By February of 2006, almost 1 of every 4 goals scored by the Capitals was by Alex Ovechkin.

Alex hopes to have a long future with his American team. "I look forward to playing many years with Washington Capitals," he says, "and my goal is to win the Stanley Cup." His teammates and fans are looking forward to that, too.

Chapter Three
Ilya Kovalchuk

Ilya Kovalchuk says he loves going to work every day. His job is left wing on the Atlanta Thrashers. Ilya shows how much he loves his work every time he scores a goal.

Ilya's Childhood

Ilya was born on April 15, 1983, in Tver, Russia. He started playing hockey at age five. Ilya remembers always being able to score goals. His father sent him to hockey school to learn basic skills.

Ilya joined the Spartak Moscow hockey club in 1999. The 2000–2001 season was his breakout year. In forty games, he scored 28 goals and had 18 assists. With Ilya's help, Spartak finished in first place in the Russian Division 1 League.

In the NHL

Ilya was the number-one pick of the Atlanta Thrashers in the first round of the 2001 draft.

Ilya fights for for the puck in a game against the Toronto Maple Leafs.

Unfortunately, Ilya missed sixteen games that season due to a shoulder injury. Still, he had 51 points, including 29 goals. This was the second highest total on the team and second among all rookies that year. He was named 2001 Rookie of the Year along with teammate Dany Heatley.

Ilya wanted to be a team leader and that meant becoming a well-rounded player. He needed to help his teammates on defense and learn to communicate on the ice. Ilya said, "I have to play not just for myself. I have to be one of the leaders on this team so I have to play hard every night." Ilya was such a good leader that NHL fans voted him 2004 Outstanding Player of the Year.

After spending the 2004–2005 lockout period in a Russian league, Ilya was ready to return to Atlanta. During the 2005–2006 season,

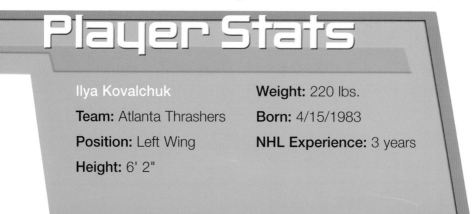

Player Stats

Ilya Kovalchuk

Team: Atlanta Thrashers

Position: Left Wing

Height: 6' 2"

Weight: 220 lbs.

Born: 4/15/1983

NHL Experience: 3 years

Ilya carries the puck ahead of teammate Marc Savard in a game against the Toronto Maple Leafs.

he led the league and his team in points and goals scored. Ilya continues to be one of the top players in the NHL.

Kovy's Kids

Ilya Kovalchuk has started a charity in Atlanta called Kovy's Kids. The organization hosts parties for kids in need. Sometimes, they play video games or go bowling, one of Ilya's favorite activities. Other times, the kids get to learn hockey skills from Ilya.

Chapter Four

Jarome Iginla

Jarome Arthur-Leigh Adekunle Tig Junior Elvis Iginla was born on July 1, 1977. Some of Jarome's names have special meaning in the Yoruba language of his Nigerian father. For example, Iginla means "big tree." Jarome was mostly raised by his American mother and grandmother in St. Albert, Alberta.

The Early Years

Jarome started his career as a goalie, but soon switched to playing right wing. He played for the St. Albert Saints in the Alberta Major Junior Hockey League. One season, he scored 34 goals in thirty-six games. He then played in the Western Hockey League of the CHL with the Kamloops Blazers of British Columbia. The team won the Memorial Cup Championship, the top prize in the CHL, in his first two seasons.

Currently playing for the Calgary Flames, Jarome shows some fancy stickhandling during a National Hockey League All-Star Game.

Drafted

Jarome entered the 1995 NHL draft and was picked eleventh overall by the Dallas Stars. The Stars let Jarome stay in Kamloops to develop his skills.

Dallas traded Jarome to Calgary for another player halfway through the 1995–1996 season. In 2001–2002, Jarome had a standout season, scoring 96 points in eighty-two games, including 52 goals. He had the highest number of points that year, receiving the Art Ross Trophy. He also had the most number of goals, for which he received the Maurice "Rocket" Richard Trophy. Jarome was the first player of African heritage to win both of these honors.

The year 2002 was also a special year for Jarome because he helped Canada win

Player Stats

Jarome Iginla

Team: Calgary Flames

Position: Right Wing

Height: 6' 1"

Weight: 208 lbs.

Born: 7/1/1977

NHL Experience: 9 years

Jarome handles the puck against the Tampa Bay Lightning during the 2004 Stanley Cup Finals.

Olympic gold. He was not originally on the Canadian team. He was called to the team when another player was injured. Jarome scored two goals in the gold medal game and became a national hero. Jarome said of his Olympic debut, "I dreamed of being on the team. But to win a gold medal and just to be with these guys . . . it means so much to me. I haven't had any better moments than this."

The Calgary Flames named Jarome team captain for the 2003–2004 season. He tied Ilya Kovalchuk and Rick Nash for the most goals scored that season. Even better, the

The Stanley Cup

The Stanley Cup was first donated in 1893 by Lord Stanley of Preston, the governor-general of Canada. It was originally given to the best Canadian amateur team. The NHL began using it as their championship trophy in 1926. The cup is awarded at the end of a series of games in which the best teams compete against each other. Today, a copy of the cup is awarded because the original cup is too fragile.

Flames went to the Stanley Cup Finals for the first time in fifteen years.

A True Leader

Jarome has said that a good hockey player obeys the rules, respects his teammates and opponents, and cares for his community. In 2004, the National Hockey League Fans' Association voted him Best Role Model. Jarome donates one thousand dollars for each goal he scores to Kidsport Calgary, an organization that helps kids to participate in sports and lead healthy lives.

Sports Trivia

- Women's hockey was played for the first time in the Olympics in 1998.
- In 1992, Canadian Manon Rhéaume became the first woman to play with the National Hockey League. She was the goalie for the Tampa Bay Lightning in a preseason game against the St. Louis Blues.

Chapter Five

Nicklas Lidstrom

After playing defense in the NHL for fourteen years, Nicklas Lidstrom knows a lot about checking opponents, scoring goals, and winning games. Year after year, he continues to be one of hockey's hottest stars.

A Talent for Hockey

Nicklas was born April 28, 1970, in Vasteras, Sweden. Although he played soccer growing up, hockey was his special talent. He played with the Vasteras hockey club before entering the 1989 NHL draft. He was chosen by the Detroit Red Wings. He played one more season in Sweden before being ready to join the Red Wings in the 1991–1992 season.

During that time, Nicklas played for the Swedish National Team. He was named one of the top three players of the 1990 World Junior Championships. Nicklas helped Sweden take the gold medal in the 1991 World Championships.

Nicklas (in red) and Ron Francis of the Carolina Hurricanes struggle for position in a Stanley Cup Finals game.

Getting His Wings

Nicklas showed he was a special defenseman during his first season with the Red Wings. That year, he was named to the All-Rookie team with 49 assists that season.

Nicklas helped the Detroit Red Wings win the Stanley Cup in 1997—their first since 1954. Nicklas was the team's top scoring defenseman and third in the league with 57 points.

Nicklas and the Red Wings won the Stanley Cup again in 1998. This time, Nicklas led all NHL defensemen with 59 points. In 2001, he won the James Norris Trophy for being the league's best defenseman. He was the first Swede to win this award. Nicklas won the award for the next two years as well! "I am happy with the overall standard of my game,

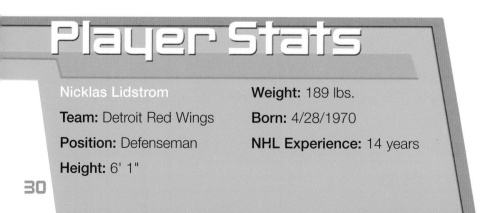

Player Stats

Nicklas Lidstrom

Team: Detroit Red Wings

Position: Defenseman

Height: 6' 1"

Weight: 189 lbs.

Born: 4/28/1970

NHL Experience: 14 years

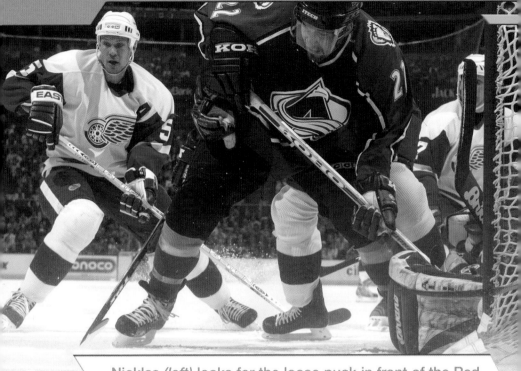

Nicklas *(left)* looks for the loose puck in front of the Red Wings goal during action against the Colorado Avalanche.

but I feel that I have the capacity to develop into an even better player," said Nicklas.

He's Got Game

On February 29, 2004, Nicklas played in his one-thousandth NHL game. He continues to be the dominant defenseman in the NHL and to hold one of the highest numbers of assists.

Chapter Six

Martin Brodeur

It seems natural that Martin Brodeur became a great goaltender. His father, Denis, was goalie for the gold medal-winning Canadian team in the 1956 Olympics. When Martin began to play hockey, however, he was a forward. Then he played backup goaltender during one tournament. The coach gave him the choice to be a forward or a goalie after that. Martin chose to be a goalie. This was the beginning of the career of one of the best goalkeepers ever to play in the NHL.

Getting Scouted

Born May 6, 1972, in Montreal, Quebec, Martin played for a minor league Montreal team in 1988–1989. In 1989, he made it into the QMJHL. He impressed NHL scouts enough to be chosen twentieth overall by the New Jersey Devils in the 1990 NHL draft. After playing a year in the American Hockey

Martin makes a big glove save in a game against the New York Rangers. Marty led the Devils to a 2–1 win.

League (AHL), the Devils asked him to be the starting goalie for the 1993–1994 season.

Martin remembers his first game, "I was nineteen, and I couldn't stop a puck in warm-up. The coaches came up to me and said, 'Don't worry, kid, just go out there and have fun.' So I did." He won that game against the Boston Bruins and twenty-seven more games that season. Martin was given the Calder Memorial Trophy in 1994 for being the NHL Rookie of the Year. The next year, Martin had 3 shutouts and helped his team win the Stanley Cup.

Score!

Martin helped the Devils return to the Stanley Cup finals. In the 1997 playoffs, Martin scored a goal against the Montreal

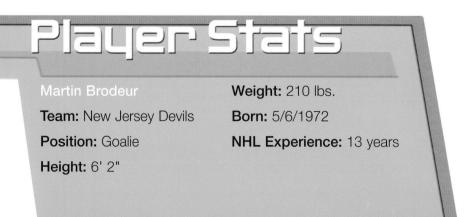

Player Stats

Martin Brodeur

Team: New Jersey Devils

Position: Goalie

Height: 6' 2"

Weight: 210 lbs.

Born: 5/6/1972

NHL Experience: 13 years

Marty's on his knees again, making a big save against Ville Nieminen of the New York Rangers.

Canadiens. This was only the fifth goal in NHL history scored by a goalie.

The New Jersey Devils won the Stanley Cup again in 2000 and 2003. Martin also won the Vezina Trophy for best goaltender in 2003 and 2004. Martin has won more than four hundred games and will most certainly win many more before he retires.

Chapter Seven
Rising Stars

There are many young players just now hitting the ice with the NHL. Most have amazing skills and talents that are already evident in their first games with the league. Those that follow are just a few of the NHL's rising stars.

Marek Svatos was drafted by the Colorado Avalanche in 2001. He made his NHL debut on October 10, 2003. Two days later, he hurt his shoulder and sat out for most of the rest of the season. When he returned to play after the NHL lockout, Marek was still considered a rookie. In the 2005–2006 season, Marek joined Crosby and Ovechkin as a top rookie in the league. Marek is a right wing. He used his skills and speed to score hat tricks, 3 goals in one game, in more than one game that year. One of Marek's teammates, Robert Blake, said of him, "You don't find many guys that want to score like that and know how." Marek is only

Marek Svatos beats his Calgary Flames opponent to the puck in a 2006 game played in Denver, Colorado.

the second rookie in Avalanche history to score a hat trick. Marek's talents were not overlooked by his countrymen in 2006, when he was chosen for the Slovakian Olympic hockey team.

Henrik Lundqvist is the top goalie in Sweden. After joining the NHL, Henrik quickly became one of the top goalies there as well. Henrik plays for the New York Rangers. He is one of only three rookies to ever have 25 saves in a season with that team. In a January 2006 game against the Florida Panthers, he made an incredible 38 saves for his second shutout game of the season. By February 2006, Henrik was ranked as the third best goalie in the NHL. Of his stellar rookie season, Henrik says, "This is a dream, to play in the [NHL] and to play for this organization. I have so much fun. So far, it's been a great year." Henrik was also a star on the Swedish team that took the gold medal at the 2006 Torino Olympic Games.

New York Rangers young goalie, Henrik Lundqvist, makes a kick save against the New York Islanders.

These rookies have already shown that they have the raw talent and skill needed to become players in the NHL. As long as they remain

Many people consider Wayne Gretzky (wearing number 99) to be the greatest hockey player of all time. Will one of today's new stars rise to the heights that the "Great One" did?

healthy and focused, the talented rookies of today will become the superstars of tomorrow.

New Words

center (**sen**-tur) a forward in middle position; the center normally takes the face-off.

checks (**cheks**) movements in which a hockey player uses his or her body or hockey stick against another player to block that player's movement

defenseman (di-**fens**-man) player whose main task is to keep opponents from scoring

dekes (**deeks**) fake moves; short for "decoy"

draft (**draft**) a system in which new players are selected for professional sports teams

face-off (**fays**-off) when a game is started by an official; a player from each team lines up as the official drops the puck

forward (**for**-wurd) a player in an attacking position

goalie (**goh**-lee) player who guards the goal

New Words

hat trick (**hat trik**) three goals in a single game

left wing (**left wing**) a forward who plays left of center

lockout (**lok**-owt) closing a business in order to resist demands of players

penalty (**pen**-uhl-tee) punishment for breaking the rules of the game

power play (**poo**-ur play) when a team has more players on the ice due to opposing team's penalties

right wing (**rite wing**) a forward who plays right of center

rookie (**ruk**-ee) new player

shutout (**shuht**-owt) a game where one team scores no points

slap shot (**slap shot**) shot in which player pulls stick back to hit the puck as hard as possible

For Further Reading

Brehm, Mike, and Michael Russo. *Rising Stars: The 10 Best Young Players in the NHL.* New York: Rosen Publishing Group, 2002.

Grabowski, John F. *The New York Rangers.* San Diego, CA: Lucent Books, 2002.

Rossiter, Sean, and Paul Carson. *Hockey: How to Play Like the Pros.* Vancouver, BC: Greystone Books, 2004.

Thomas, Keltie. *How Hockey Works.* Toronto: Maple Tree Press, 2002.

Wilson, Stacy. *The Hockey Book for Girls.* Toronto: Kids Can Press, 2000.

Resources

Resources

WEB SITES

Hockey Hall of Fame
http://www.hhof.com
Learn more about hockey, its players, and its
history on this informative site.

National Hockey League Kids Web Site
http://www.nhl.com/kids
This Web site has cool games to play online,
video highlights of your favorite players, and
fun hockey facts. You can even ask hockey
legend Willie O'Ree questions about the game.

USA Hockey: Girls and Women
http://www.usahockey.com/girlswomen/
Find out more about the growing number of
girls playing ice hockey and locate a team in
your area on this site.

Index

A
assists,12, 19, 30–31
Atlanta Thrashers,19–20

B
Brodeur, Martin, 33–35

C
Calgary Flames, 24, 26
Canada, 9, 24 26
Canadian Hockey League (CHL), 9–10, 12, 23
center, 6, 9–10
checks, 6
Colorado Avalanche, 37
Crosby, Sidney, 10–13

D
Dallas Stars, 24
defenseman, 5–6, 15, 30–31
dekes, 6
Detroit Red Wings, 30
draft, 10, 12, 17, 19, 24, 29, 33, 37

F
face-off, 6
fans, 12, 17, 20, 27
forward, 17, 33

G
goalie, 5¬6, 23, 27, 33–35, 38–39
goals, 10, 12, 17, 19–21, 23–24, 26, 29, 37

H
hat trick, 16, 37–38

I
Iginla, Jarome, 24–27

K
Kovalchuk, Ilya, 19–21, 26

L
left wing, 5–6, 16, 19–20
Lidstrom, Nicklas, 29–31
lockout, 12, 17, 20, 37
Lundqvist, Henrik, 38–39

M
Moscow Dynamo, 16

N
National Hockey League (NHL), 9–10, 12–13, 16–17,19–21, 24, 26–27, 29–31, 33–35, 37–38, 40
New Jersey Devils, 34–35
New York Rangers, 38–39

Index

ABOUT THE AUTHOR

Therese Shea lives and writes in Buffalo, New York. A graduate of Providence College and the State University of New York at Buffalo, she is the author of several books.